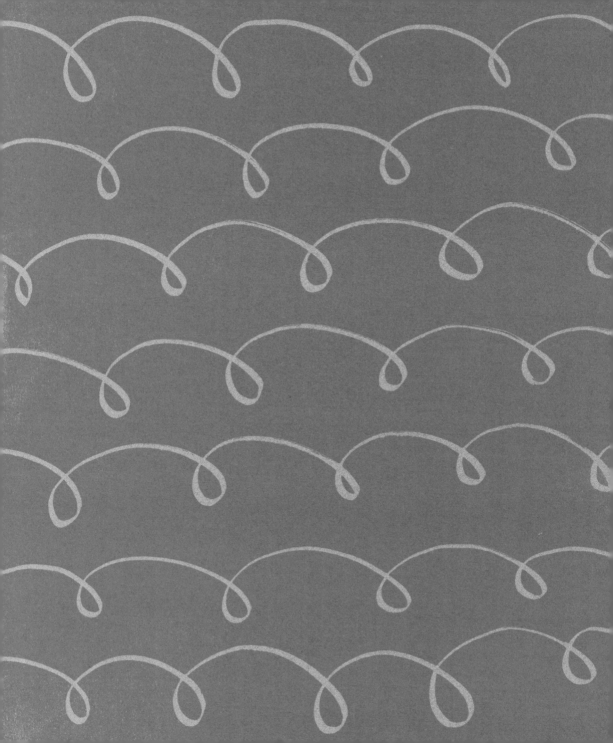

I wrote
a book about
you

Dear _____,

I wrote a Book about you. But you helped.
A lot. Because you're you. (Which means
I obviously had some great material
to work with.) So it was easy to come up
with lots to say about the incredible
person you are, the wonderful things
you do, and all the ways you are completely,
Ridiculously, perfectly unlike anyone else.

And you know what? It turned out to
Be a pretty good Book. (And not just
Because I wrote it.) It's good because
you're you. And because that (in my Book)
is pretty much the BEST.

Yours,

_____

I've put some thought into this and I just wanted to tell you that, honestly,

It's kind of
CRAZY how

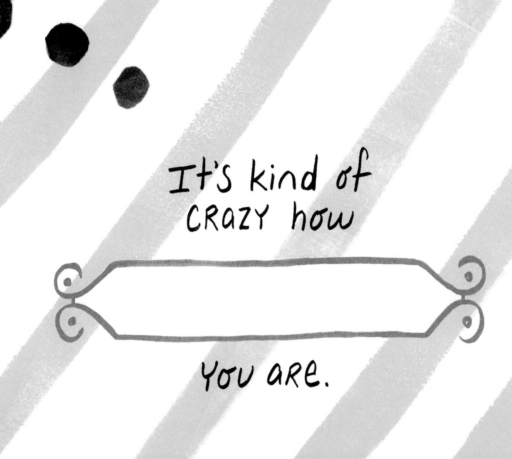

YOU aRe.

You are always completely and effortlessly

I KNOW it doesn't qualify as a SUPERPOWER exactly, but...

I think
YOUR aBILITY TO

is PRETTY
RemarKaBLe.

THERE are a few things

ABOUT YOU THAT *I know* for SURE.

If you were an **ANIMAL**, you'd be:

And if you were a **COLOR**, you'd be:

If you were a **SOUP**, you'd be:

And if you were a **SUPERHERO**, you'd be:

Here's a *little* CELEBRATION of one of my faVORite things about you,

which is
(of course)
your

One of the
Very most
WONDERFUL
THINGS ABOUT HAVING
YOU IN MY LIFE IS
GETTING TO SEE YOU

WHEN I TALK about you to people You've never met, I DESCRIBE YOU AS:

In my dream world there's a VACATION I get to take you on, and it LOOKS LIKE THIS

I've packed a BaG of YouR favoRite snacks, Like _____ and _____. Here's where we'RE GoinG: _____.

While we aRe theRe, we'll stay in _____, with a view of _____. We'll spend ouR time _____, _____, and _____.

One thing in our
▸ PRESENT ◂
I hope we get to
HAVE FOREVER

One thing in our
◄ FUTURE ►
I can't wait to
MAKE HAPPEN

Whether or not you always let yourself BELieve it,

You're REALLY
incredibly

You know what never fails to make me smile?

Thinking about
that time we

If I created a sandwich for you,
here's what would be on it:

If I made you a T-shirt, this is
what it would say:

If I had to sing a karaoke song
for you (and you alone), it would be:

And if I could give you a TROPHY, IT WOULD BE FOR

I, for one, am really GRATEFUL that you

So much.

(Truly. Thank you.)

after DOING extensive RESEARCH, I'm almost 100% certain of this:

you're probably
THE MOST

PERSON I KNOW.

I won't tell anyone,
But I happen to KNOW
that you are secretly
= powered by a =
COMBINATION OF:

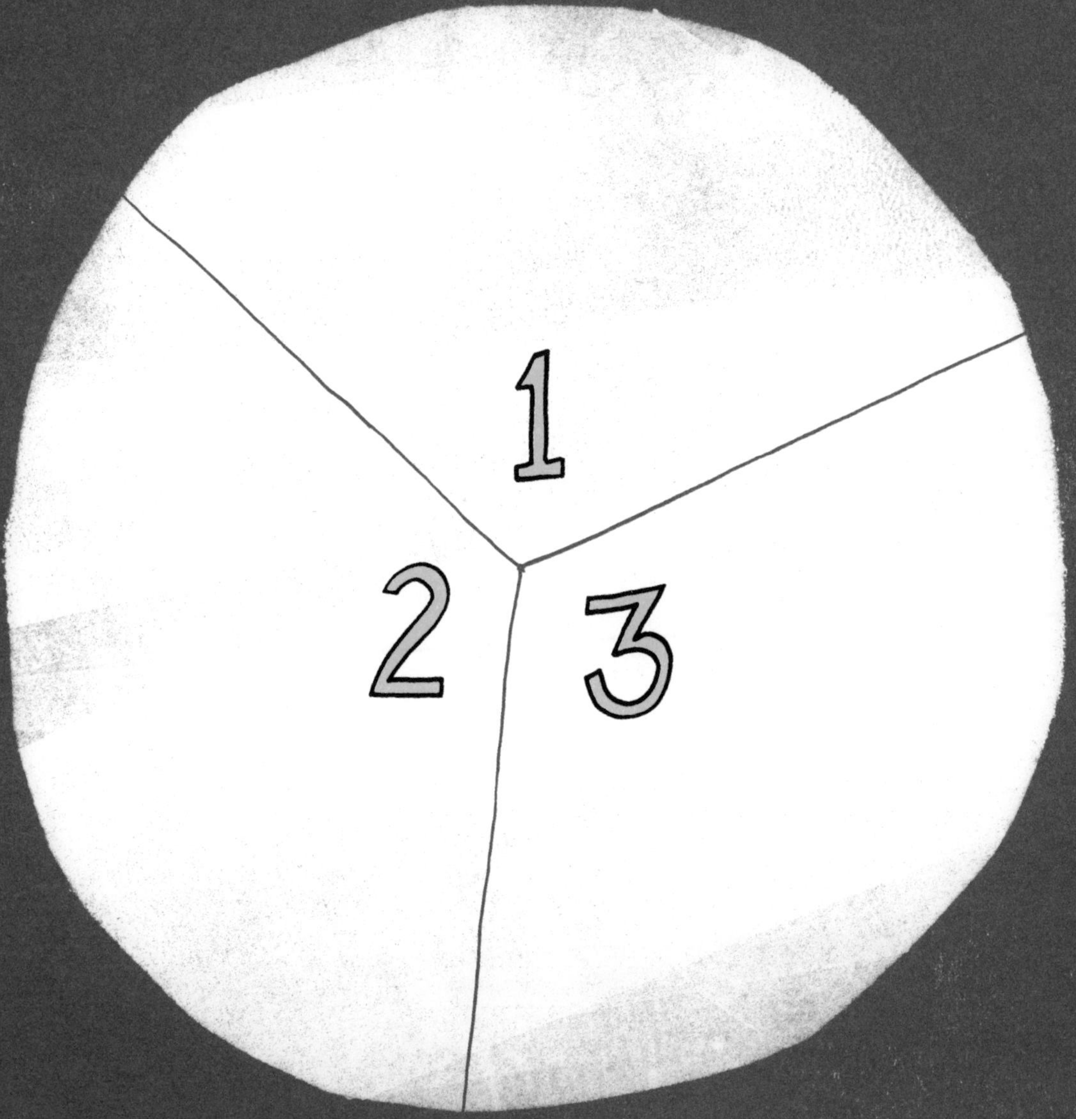
1
2
3

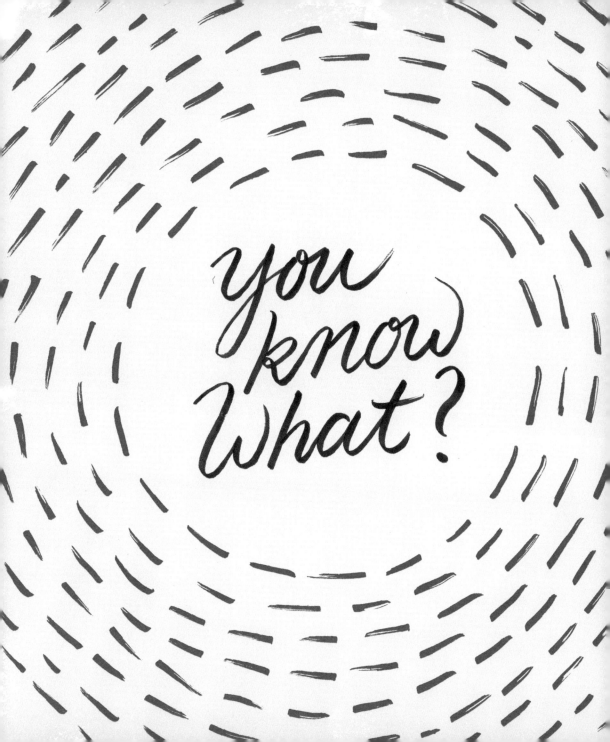

You are the only person I know
who can do this:

You are the only person I know
who likes this:

And you are definitely the only
person I know who can get away with:

No matter howMANY MILLIONS of people there ARE in the WORLD, I'm certain OF THIS:

no one will EVER be able to duplicate your

I THINK it would be ABSOLUTELY IMPOSSIBLE for anyone who's known you for any time at all NOT TO NOTICE...

Which is WHY You're
even cute when YOU:

If TIME travel technology ever gets really good, there are So MANY MOMENTS and places we should GO BACK TO.

I think some of the first things
we'd have to Relive would be...

The day we:

The time we:

and when we:

As far as I know,
You've NEVER TRIED IT, BUT...

I Bet you'd BE a

=WORLD-CLASS=

If I had the ⚡ POWER to rearrange the WORLD just a little bit, I would:

Make sure you got to spend
much MORE time

AND
much Less Time

You do so much GOOD in so many ways, ALL day, EVERY DAY, But if I had to pick just ONE THING, I'd say:

═ IS YOUR ═
GREATEST GIFT
to the world.

So. I THINK you should know that Sometimes, there are MOMENTS when I'm COMPLETELY BOWLED OVER By how much I love having you in My LIFE.

Here's one. We were here:

And this was happening:

And I found myself thinking:

HAVING YOU in my life has ABSOLUTELY MADE ME:

More ▢

And less ▢

And just ▢
▢ in general.

I PROBABLY don't TELL YOU this enough, BUT the ONE THING I want you to ALWAYS, always know is:

COMPENDIUM.
live inspired

Actually
Written By:
— — — — —

WRITTEN BY: M.H. Clark

DESIGNED & ILLUSTRATED BY: Justine Edge

EDITED BY: Ruth Austin

ISBN: 978-1-943200-10-8

20th printing. Printed in China with soy and metallic inks on FSC®-Mix certified paper.

Create meaningful moments with gifts that inspire.

CONNECT WITH US
live-inspired.com | sayhello@compendiuminc.com

@compendiumliveinspired
#compendiumliveinspired

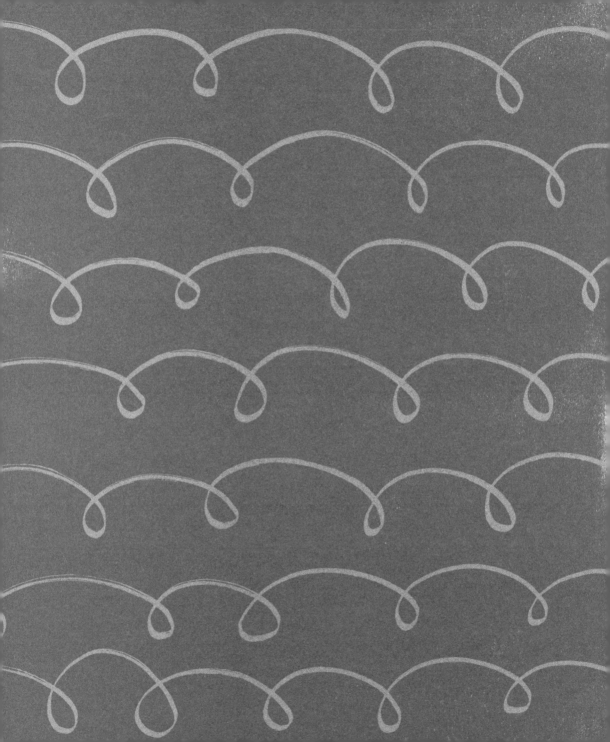